Let's Make MUSIC

The Drum

and Other Percussion Instruments

Rita Storey

A+

Smart Apple Media

Smart Apple Media
P.O. Box 3263, Mankato, Minnesota 56002

Printed in the United States

Published by arrangement with the Watts Publishing Group Ltd, London.

Art director: Jonathan Hair
Series designed and created for Franklin Watts by Painted Fish Ltd.
Designer: Rita Storey
Editor: Fiona Corbridge
Adviser: Helen MacGregor

Picture credits
Corbis/Jeremy Bembaron p. 23; istockphoto.com pp. 8, 10, 12, 14 (bottom), 15,
16, 17, 21 (top), 26, 28 (bottom); Odile Noel/Redferns p. 15, Toby Wales/Redferns
p. 25; Tudor Photography pp. 3, 4, 5, 6, 7, 9, 11, 13, 14 (top), 18, 19, 20, 21 (bottom
left and right), 23, 28 (top); Ulster Orchestra p. 24.

Cover images: Tudor Photography, Banbury

All photos posed by models.
Thanks to Husnen Ahmad, Serena Donnelly, Maddi Indun, George Stapleton,
Hannah Storey, and Natasha Vinall

Library of Congress Cataloging-in-Publication Data

Storey, Rita.
  The drum and other percussion instruments / Rita Storey.
     p. cm. -- (Let's make music)
  Includes index.
  Summary: "Introduces different percussion instruments and the ways they are
played, providing do-it-yourself crafts and activities"--Provided by the publisher."
  ISBN 978-1-59920-214-3 (hardcover)
  1. Percussion instruments--Juvenile literature. 2. Drum--Juvenile literature. I.
Title.
  ML1030.S76 2010
  786.9--dc22
                              2008040683

Contents

Words in **bold** are in the glossary.

The Drum

A drum is a musical instrument made from a frame with a drumhead stretched over it.

The drum is part of the **percussion** family.

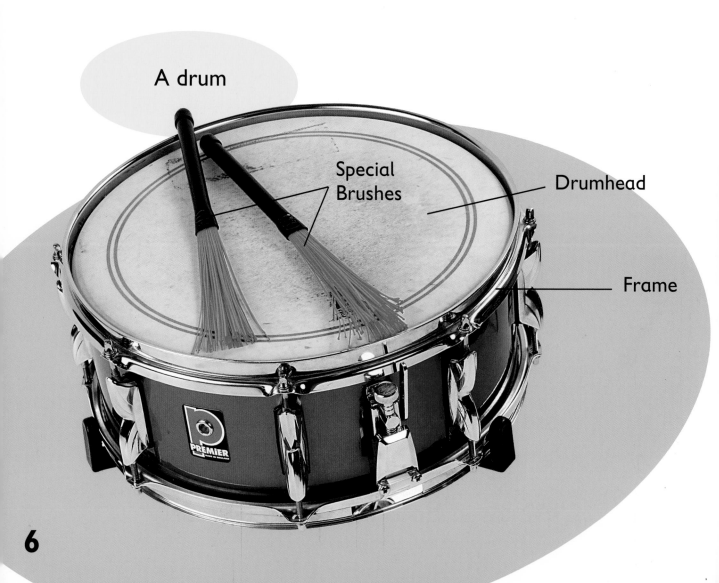

A drum

Special Brushes

Drumhead

Frame

Making a Sound

To make a sound with a drum, tap or beat it with your hands, drumsticks, a **mallet,** or special brushes.

You can play drums standing up, sitting down, or even as you march along.

This boy is playing a drum using drumsticks.

Listen!
Pages 27 and 28 tell you about music played on percussion instruments that you can listen to.

Drumsticks

The sound

When you tap or beat the drumhead, it shakes very fast. It is vibrating.

Vibrations

When the drum skin vibrates, it makes the air around it also move. These **vibrations** in the air are called **sound waves**.

When you play a drum, some of the sound waves go down into the hollow body of the drum. This makes the sounds louder.

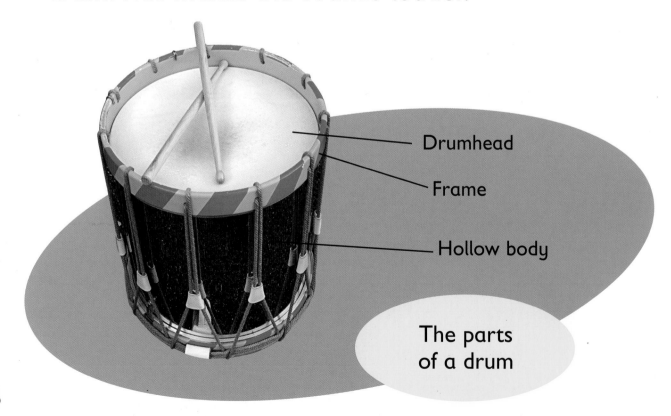

Drumhead

Frame

Hollow body

The parts of a drum

Try This

Make a drum by stretching a piece of plastic over a bowl. Hold it in place with an elastic band. The plastic must be tight.

Using pencils as drumsticks, play the drum. Sound waves make the sound that you hear.

Put a few grains of rice on the drum and play it again. Can you see the rice moving as the drumhead vibrates?

High and Low

Drums are made in different sizes and from different materials. Each one has a different overall sound.

Drum Sounds and Sizes

Some sounds are high and some are low. We say they have a high **pitch** or a low pitch.

A small drum has a high pitch. A large drum has a low pitch.

This big drum has a very low pitch.

The way you hit a drum (hard or gently), and what you hit it with, affects the sound it makes.

A drum set is a set of drums and **cymbals** of different sizes. It has a foot pedal to work the hi-hat cymbals and another to make a **beater** hit the bass drum.

Crash cymbal

Tom-toms

Hi-hat cymbals

Snare drum

Floor tom

Bass drum

Playing a drum set

The Beat

Drums are used to give a regular beat to a piece of music.

Playing the drums in a marching band

Drums are popular in **marching bands**. The regular beat of a drum tells the members of the band when to take a step.

A **drummer** may play a different beat or rhythm with each hand and each foot.

Try This

Try tapping a regular beat (**1–2**, **1–2**) with a pencil on the table. Now tap a rhythm (**1–2**, **1–2–3**, **1–2**, **1–2–3**) with your other hand. Can you do both things together?

Playing a beat and a rhythm at the same time is very hard.

Shapes and Sizes ♫

Here are some more drums.
They make different
sounds because of
their shape, the
materials they are
made of, and the way
they are played.

Hourglass
The laces can
be squeezed
together to
change the
sound on
this drum.

Taiko
Japanese taiko
drums are shaped
like a barrel. They
are played with
drumsticks and
make a very
deep sound.

Timpani

These drums are shaped like bowls. They are very big and make a loud sound. They are played in an **orchestra**.

Bodhran

This Irish drum is open at the back. It is held in one hand and played very fast with a wooden stick.

Djembe

This drum comes from Africa. It is played with bare hands. The bottom of the drum rests on the ground.

Percussion

These shakers are unpitched percussion instruments.

Percussion instruments are a group of instruments that make sounds when you hit or tap them, scrape them, or shake them.

They are often used to play the rhythm of a piece of music.

The sound they make depends on what they are made of and the way that you play them.

Unpitched Percussion

These are simple instruments. They may be made of materials such as wood, seed pods, and gourds. The sounds they make do not have a fixed pitch—we say they are unpitched.

Pitched Percussion

Some percussion instruments are tuned so that you can play musical notes. These are called pitched instruments.

Music Notes

To be able to play music that other people have made up, or composed, you need to understand how to read music.

Music is written in musical notes. **Symbols** tell us how long or short a note is. Notes are named after letters: A, B, C, D, E, F, G. The length of the notes in a piece of music make up its rhythm.

The notes are written on five lines called a staff. The place of a note on the staff tells us its pitch—how high or low it is.

A B C D E F G

The marimba is a pitched percussion instrument. Each wooden bar plays a different note. The tubes below make the notes louder.

Shake and Rattle

The percussion instruments on these pages are played by shaking them.

Maracas

Maracas have a hard outer shell made of leather, wood, or plastic. There are dried seeds inside that make sound when you shake them.

Maracas come from South America.

Make a Simple Shaker

Put a few pieces of dried macaroni noodles into a small plastic bottle, then put the cap on. Shake it and listen to the sound. How is the sound different if you put rice grains into the bottle instead?

All these instruments are shaken to make sounds.

Cabassa
This rattle is covered in beads. It comes from Brazil.

Castanets
These make a "click-clack" sound. They come from Spain.

Sleigh Bells
These bells are fixed to a wooden handle. They jingle when you shake them.

19

Beat It

Here are some percussion instruments that you play by tapping, beating, or scraping them.

Tambourine

A tambourine is like a small, light drum that you hold in the air. You play it by tapping it with your other hand, or by shaking it. It has metal discs called jingles in the frame.

Playing a tambourine.

Jingles
These make a ringing sound when you tap or shake the tambourine.

Bongos

These drums are joined together. You play them with your hands. One has a higher pitch than the other.

Bongos

Tap and Scrape

A triangle is a rod of steel bent into a triangle shape. You tap it with a metal stick. An agogo is made of wood. It is played by scraping a stick along its ridges.

Playing a triangle

An Agogo

More Percussion

You can use some strange things as percussion instruments.

Stomp

Stomp is a music and dance show. The performers use brooms, trash can lids and kitchen **utensils** as percussion instruments.

Stomp performers using brooms to tap out rhythms.

A Percussion Band

To start a percussion band, look for things that you think might make good percussion instruments. Try to find things that will make different sounds. Ask your friends to do the same.

Decide on a beat and a rhythm, then start playing percussion!

Trash can lids and a cheese-grater played with a whisk make very different sounds.

The Orchestra

Both pitched and unpitched percussion instruments are played in an orchestra.

A Percussionist

A person who plays a percussion instrument is called a percussionist. The percussionist in an orchestra plays lots of different instruments.

Timpani

The pitch of these drums can be changed by pressing a foot pedal to make the drum skin tighter or looser.

Playing a timpani

This percussionist has lots of different instruments to play.

Unusual Percussion

Percussion instruments can be used for special effects that add to the **atmosphere** of a piece of music. They can sound like thunder, sleigh bells, or even frogs croaking.

Some composers include very unusual percussion instruments in their music. To make a sound like rain, the musician strings together a row of teacups and taps them.

Different Styles

Percussion instruments can be used to play many different styles of music.

Steel Pans

Steel oil drums can be turned into drums called pans. They are tuned to produce notes.

Steel drums are used to play Caribbean music.

This drummer is playing rock music.

Rock Music

Rock music is another style of music. It is often loud and fast.

Listen!

Web Sites

Drums

Be a drummer and play a whole range of drums and cymbals by rolling the mouse or using the keypad on the virtual drum set at:
http://www.kenbrashear.com

See Animal from *The Muppets* play a drum set with the famous American drummer, Buddy Rich at:
http://www.drummerworld.com/drummers/Animal.html

Watch videos of many exciting drum performances at:
http://www.drummerworld.com/drummervideo.html

Learn about Japanese taiko drums, listen to the music, see pictures of them and watch a thrilling video of a taiko performance at:
http://www.taiko.org/kidsweb/index.html

Percussion

Hear music that features several orchestral percussion instruments including cymbals, timpani, xylophone and bass drum at:
http://www.playmusic.org/percussion/index.html

Read about the history of some uncommon percussion instruments. Hear sound clips of them being played in the early 1900s, and view posters of the strange instruments being advertised at:
http://www.americaslibrary.gov/cgi-bin/page.cgi/sh/oddball/mallet_1

Watch the *Stomp* performers in action. See the different objects they use to create rhythms. Highlight on "the show" link and click on "video and audio clips" at: *http://www.stomponline.com*

CDs

Britten: *Young Person's Guide to the Orchestra.*

Bela Bartok: *Sonata for Two Pianos and Percussion.*

Leonard Bernstein: *Symphonic Dances from West Side Story.*

James MacMillan: *Veni, Veni Emmanuel* (percussion concerto played by percussionist Colin Currie).

Steve Reich: *Drumming.*

Stomp: *Stomp Out Loud* (DVD of performances).

Madou Djembe: *African Drums.*

Palghat Raghu: *Impressions* (double-headed drum and tabla from India).

Gong Kebyar: *The Earth Meets the Sun* (gamelan music from Bali).

Glossary

Atmosphere Feeling or mood.

Beater Something used to strike an instrument.

Cymbal A piece of metal that produces a sharp, ringing sound when you hit it with a drumstick.

Drummer A person who plays the drums.

Drumhead A piece of plastic or skin held inside a drum frame, or stretched tightly over it.

Frame The body of a drum that holds the drumhead.

Mallet A type of hammer.

Marching band A group of musicians who play their instruments while they march in formation.

Orchestra A large group of performers playing various musical instruments.

Percussion A group of instruments that make sounds when you tap them, scrape them or shake them.

Pitch A high musical note or sound is said to have a high pitch. A low musical note or sound is said to have a low pitch.

Sound wave A wave that transmits sound through the air.

Symbol A shape used to represent something else.

Utensil A tool, or a simple machine.

Vibrating; vibration Moving back and forth rapidly.

Index